"DOMINATING JAVASCRIPT: REVEALING THE FORCE OF WEB IMPROVEMENT"

Contents

4

Introduction:

Momentarily make sense of what JavaScript is and its significance in web improvement. Notice the ideal interest group, which are fledglings with practically no coding experience.

JavaScript is an imperative part of present-day web improvement, and it assumes a significant part in upgrading the intelligence and usefulness of sites. As an essayist and distributer taking special care of novices with restricted coding experience, giving a reasonable and compact clarification of JavaScript is fundamental.

JavaScript is a flexible programming language used to make dynamic and intuitive components on sites. Not at all like HTML and CSS, are which fundamentally answerable for organizing and styling web content, has JavaScript added conduct to site pages. It empowers you to fabricate highlights like picture sliders, structure approval, and intuitive guides, making sites seriously captivating and easy to understand.

For novices in the realm of web improvement, JavaScript is an extraordinary beginning stage in light of its easy-to-understand punctuation and an abundance of online assets. Its significance couldn't possibly be more significant, as it enables designers to rejuvenate static website pages, making a more vivid and connecting client experience.

In this guide focused on fledglings, we'll dive further into JavaScript, investigating its essential ideas, linguistic structure, and useful applications. By and by, you'll have a strong groundwork to begin integrating JavaScript into your web improvement projects, making your sites more powerful and interesting to your crowd.

Getting everything moving with JavaScript

What is JavaScript?

Setting up an improvement environment (code editor and program).
Your most significant JavaScript program: "Hello, World!"

JavaScript is an adaptable and comprehensively elaborate programming language that expects a critical part in web improvement. As a writer and distributer, you'll track down it particularly significant for working on your webpage and online substance. We ought to dive into the nuances of getting everything going with JavaScript.

What is JavaScript?

JavaScript is an obvious level, translated programming language essentially known for adding instinct to locales. Making dynamic and responsive web applications is often used. JavaScript have some control over the substance of a page, handle client joint efforts, and even talk with servers in the background. Its adaptability makes it a basic instrument for present day web improvement.

Setting up an improvement environment

Before you can start forming JavaScript code, you'll require a sensible improvement environment. You need this:

Code Manager: You can investigate a grouping of code editors, for instance, Visual Studio Code, Splendid Text, or Particle. These editors give sentence structure highlighting, code culmination, and investigating gadgets to make your coding experience more pleasing.

Browser: Since JavaScript runs in web programs, it's basic to have one presented. Notable choices consolidate Google Chrome, Mozilla Firefox, and Microsoft Edge. Originators often use program engineer instruments to test and investigate their JavaScript code.

Your most noteworthy JavaScript program: " Hello, World!"
We ought to make an essential "Howdy, World!" program in JavaScript to start. This praiseworthy model is the underlying step for any programmer:

```javascript
Copy code
// Make a capacity to show a message
capacity sayHello() {
  alert("Hello, World!");
}


// Call the capacity
sayHello();
```

In this code, we portray a capacity alluded to sayHello that shows a wariness with the message as "Hello, World!" when called. The sayHello() capacity is summoned close to the end, which sets off the mindfulness to jump up in your web program when you run the code.

As you continue with your journey with JavaScript, you'll research factors, circles, prohibitive announcements, and more muddled applications. JavaScript's capacities are huge, and it might be used to make everything from natural designs to dynamic web games.

Remember, as a writer and distributer, you can use JavaScript to make your locales truly enthralling and straightforward. You can make instinctive substance,

collect client analysis, and further develop the overall client experience. A huge mastery can isolate your online disseminations.
Factors and Their Utilization

In JavaScript, factors resemble compartments that hold various kinds of information. They are a key idea in programming and are fundamental for putting away and controlling data. Consider them marked boxes where you can keep things.

To proclaim a variable in JavaScript, you utilize the var, let, or const watchword, trailed by the variable name. Here is a model:

javascript

Duplicate code

var age = 30;// Pronounce a variable 'age' and dole out it the worth 30

You can change the worth of a variable whenever:

javascript
Duplicate code
age = 31;// Update the 'age' variable to 31
Information Types in JavaScript

JavaScript upholds a few information types:

Numbers: Utilized for numeric qualities, the two numbers and decimals.

javascript
Duplicate code
var cost = 19.99;// A variable 'cost' with a numeric worth
Strings: Utilized for printed information, encased in single or twofold statements.

javascript
Duplicate code
var name = "Alice";// A variable 'name' with a string esteem
Booleans: Utilized for valid or bogus qualities.

javascript

Duplicate code

```
var isStudent = valid;// A variable 'isStudent' with a boolean worth
```

Exhibits: Used to store arrangements of values.

javascript
Duplicate code

```
var organic products = ["apple", "banana", "cherry"];// A variety of strings
```

Objects: Used to store key-esteem matches, giving an organized method for coordinating information.

javascript
Duplicate code

```
var individual = {
  name: " Sway",
  age: 25
};
```

Variable Naming Shows

It's critical to follow naming shows for factors to compose spotless and justifiable code. Here are a few normal practices:

Variable names ought to be engaging, showing the reason for the variable.
Use camelCase for variable names (e.g., myVariableName) for further developed intelligibility.
Begin variable names with a letter (A-Z or a-z) or a highlight (_).
Try not to utilize held words or catchphrases (e.g., var, capability) as factor names.
Here is a model with legitimate naming shows:

javascript
Duplicate code

```
var firstName = "John";// Illustrative variable name utilizing camelCase
```

Understanding factors and information types is key in JavaScript, as it frames the reason for working with information and making dynamic applications. These ideas permit you to store, control, and cycle data in your projects.

Number juggling Administrators:

In JavaScript, number-crunching administrators are the central apparatuses for performing numerical activities. The fundamental ones incorporate expansion (+), deduction (-), augmentation (*), and division (/). For instance, you can utilize the + administrator to add two numbers, the - administrator to deduct, * to increase, and/to partition. Here is a model:

javascript
Duplicate code

```
let a = 5;
let b = 3;
let total = a + b; // This will bring about 'aggregate' containing 8.
```

Examination Administrators:

Correlation administrators are utilized to look at values. In JavaScript, normal ones incorporate more prominent than (>), not exactly (<), and triple equivalents (===) for severe uniformity. The > administrator checks in the event that the worth on the left is more prominent than the one on the right, < checks assuming it's less, and === checks on the off chance that they are totally equivalent. For example:

javascript
Duplicate code
let x = 10;
let y = 5;
let isGreater = x > y; // This will be valid, as 10 is more prominent than 5.

Legitimate Administrators:

Consistent administrators in JavaScript are utilized for consolidating or discrediting articulations. There are legitimate AND (&&), sensible OR (||), and coherent NOT (!). They are many times utilized in restrictive proclamations. Here is a model:

javascript
Duplicate code
let hasMoney = valid;
let isSunny = misleading;

```
let goOutside = hasMoney && isSunny; // This checks assuming the two circumstances are valid prior to heading outside.
```

Involving Articulations in JavaScript:

JavaScript articulations are mixes of values, factors, and administrators that can be assessed to a solitary worth. These are the structure blocks for more mind boggling rationale in your code. For example:

javascript
Duplicate code
let span = 5;
let region = Math. PI * (span * range); // This works out the region of a circle with a given range.
In synopsis, understanding and really utilizing these administrators and articulations are vital for programming in JavaScript. They empower you to perform computations, decide, and control the progression of your code.
Contingent Clarifications:

Prohibitive clarifications are a significant piece of programming in JavaScript. They grant you to execute different code blocks considering decided conditions. The chief kinds are:

if: This declaration truly takes a gander at a condition, and if it's legitimate, it executes the code inside the block. For example:

```javascript
Copy code
if (condition) {
  // Code to run when the condition
is substantial.
}
```

else if and else: These are used to give elective code blocks when the basic condition (or past conditions) is fake.

javascript
Copy code
```javascript
if (condition1) {
  // Code to run when condition1 is substantial.
} else if (condition2) {
  // Code to run when condition2 is legitimate.
} else {
  // Code to run when no conditions are met.
}
```

Switch Clarifications:

Switch enunciations are another strategy for dealing with various conditions. They are particularly useful when you have a lone worth to take a gander at against various cases. Here is a model:

javascript
Copy code
```javascript
switch (regard) {
```

```
  case 1:
    // Code for case 1
    break;
  case 2:
    // Code for case 2
    break;
  default:
    // Code to run if none of the cases match
}
```

Circles:

Circles are major for dismal endeavors in programming. JavaScript gives two essential sorts:

for circles: These are used when you know how much of the time you want to repeat a block of code.

javascript
Copy code
```
for (let I = 0; i < 5; i++) {
```

```
  // Code to reiterate on numerous occasions
}
```

while circles: These are useful when you want to go over a block of code up to a condition is legitimate.

javascript
Copy code

```
while (condition) {
  // Code to reiterate for whatever length of time condition is substantial
}
```

Working with Bunches and Circles:

Groups are arrangements of data in JavaScript. You can use circles to stress through the parts of a bunch. For instance, to circle through a display and play out a movement on each part:

javascript
Copy code

```
 // Access each part using myArray[i]
  // Code to deal with each part
}
```

Then again, you can use a for...of circle for a cleaner and more clear technique for rehashing through bunches:

javascript
Copy code

```
for (const part of myArray) {
  // Code to manage each part
}
```

I trust this information helps you in your structure and disseminating work. If you truly need more nuances on any of these subjects or have express requests, generously feel free to ask.

Characterizing Capabilities and Their Significance:

In JavaScript, a capability is a block of code that can be named and reused. They assume a significant part in putting together and modularizing your code. Capabilities permit you to epitomize a particular piece of usefulness, making your code more lucid and viable. You characterize a capability utilizing the capability catchphrase, trailed by a name and a bunch of enclosures. For instance:

```javascript
Duplicate code
capability greet(name) {
  return "Hi, " + name + "!";
}
```

Boundaries and Contentions in Capabilities:

Boundaries are like placeholders for values that you need to pass into a capability. In the model above, name is a boundary. At the point when you call the capability, you give genuine qualities that are called contentions. For example:

javascript
Duplicate code
let message = greet("Alice");
For this situation, "Alice" is the contention for the name boundary. It's the way you pass information to a capability for it to work with.

Bring Proclamations back:

The return explanation is utilized to indicate what a capability ought to offer back subsequently. It's discretionary yet fundamental in the event that you believe your capability should deliver some result. For instance:

```javascript
Duplicate code
capability add(a, b) {
  return a + b;
}
let outcome = add(5, 3);// result is currently 8
```

Extension and Variable Perceivability in JavaScript:

Scope characterizes where factors are available. JavaScript has two principal scopes: worldwide and neighborhood. Factors pronounced beyond any capability are worldwide and can be gotten to from anyplace in your code. Factors proclaimed inside a capability are neighborhood and must be utilized inside that capability.

javascript
Duplicate code

```
let globalVar = "I'm worldwide";

capability exampleFunction() {
  let localVar = "I'm nearby";
  console.log(globalVar);//      This works
  console.log(localVar);      // This works as well
}

console.log(globalVar);//      This works
```

```
console.log(localVar);   // This will bring about a mistake
```

Understanding these ideas is essential to composing effective and viable JavaScript code, which is especially significant while you're composing scripts for your distributing or composing projects.

Articles and Clusters in JavaScript:

In JavaScript, articles and clusters are fundamental information structures used to sort out and control information.

Objects:

An item in JavaScript is an assortment of key-esteem matches. It's a flexible information structure that can hold different information types.

You can make an article utilizing wavy supports like this:

javascript

Duplicate code

```
let individual = {
    name: " John",
    age: 30,
    calling: " Author"
```

```
};
```

Access values inside an article utilizing spot documentation (person.name) or section documentation (person['name']).
Arrays:

A cluster is an arranged rundown of values. In JavaScript, exhibits can contain a blend of various information types.
You can make an exhibit utilizing square sections like this:
javascript
Duplicate code

```
let tones = ["red", "green", "blue"];
```

Access components in a cluster utilizing their file, beginning from 0 (e.g., colors[0] would give you "red").
Making and Working with Items:

To make an article, characterize it utilizing wavy supports and populate it with key-esteem matches.

You can add, adjust, or erase properties in an article utilizing spot documentation or section documentation.

For instance, to add another property:

javascript

Duplicate code

person.city = "New York";

To eliminate a property:

javascript

Duplicate code

erase person.profession;

Making and Working with Clusters:

Make an exhibit by characterizing it with square sections and populating it with values.

You can add, eliminate, or alter components in an exhibit.

To add a component toward the finish of a cluster:

javascript

Duplicate code

colors.push("yellow");

To eliminate the last component:

javascript

Duplicate code

colors.pop();

1. Object-Situated Programming (OOP) Rudiments:

2. Object-situated writing computer programs is a programming worldview that utilizes objects to structure and address information and conduct. Key OOP ideas include:

3. Classes and Articles: Classes characterize plans for endlessly protests are occasions of classes.
4. Inheritance: Subclasses can acquire properties and strategies from a parent class.
5. Encapsulation: Packaging information and strategies into objects, concealing the inside subtleties from an external perspective.
6. Polymorphism: Objects of various classes can be treated as objects of a typical superclass.
7. In JavaScript, you can carry out OOP utilizing models or more present day ES6 classes.

8. I trust this gives an extensive outline of items, clusters, and OOP in JavaScript for your

composition and distributing needs. Assuming you want more point by point data or have explicit inquiries, go ahead and inquire.

Prologue to the Report Item Model (DOM)

The Report Item Model, regularly alluded to as the DOM, is a major idea in web improvement. It addresses the construction of a site page as a various leveled tree of articles, permitting us to get to and control the substance and design of a site page. Fundamentally, it fills in as a delegate between the substance of a site page and the programming dialects used to connect with it, like JavaScript.

Job of the DOM in Web Advancement

The DOM assumes a vital part in web improvement in light of multiple factors:

Openness of Web Content: It gives an organized portrayal of the site page's substance, making it open to contents and programming dialects. This openness is the establishment for dynamic web applications.

Dynamic Substance Control: With the DOM, you can progressively change the substance and design of a website page without requiring a full page invigorate. This is fundamental for making intelligent and responsive web applications.

UI Intuitiveness: It considers occasion taking care of, empowering the production of intelligent UIs. Occasions like snaps, mouse developments, and console data sources can set off activities, making web applications seriously captivating.

Information Recovery and Accommodation: The DOM empowers information recovery from web structures and accommodation to servers. This is a center piece of client cooperation's, for example, submitting structures or collaborating with data sets.

Choosing and Controlling HTML Components Utilizing JavaScript

- JavaScript is the essential language used to cooperate with the DOM. This is the way you can choose and control HTML components with JavaScript:

- Choosing Components: You can choose components utilizing techniques like getElementById, getElementsByClassName, or query Selector to target explicit components on the page.

- Adjusting Content: When a component is chosen, you can change its substance, credits, and styling utilizing JavaScript. For instance, changing the text of a passage or refreshing the foundation shade of a div.

- Making Components: You can make new components and add them to the page. This is helpful for progressively producing content.

Occasion Taking care of with JavaScript

- Occasion dealing with is a basic part of web improvement. JavaScript permits you to answer client collaborations through occasion audience members.

This is the closely guarded secret:

- Adding Occasion Audience members: You can append occasion audience members to HTML components to tune in for occasions like snaps, key presses, or mouse developments.

- Occasion Taking care of Capabilities: At the point when an occasion happens, a JavaScript capability is executed. This capability can perform different activities, from straightforward cautions to complex information handling.

- Forestalling Default Activities: You can likewise forestall the default conduct of occasions. For instance, keeping a structure from submitting when a button is clicked.

- All in all, the DOM is the foundation of web improvement, furnishing an organized method for collaborating with and control web content. JavaScript is the essential language utilized for this reason, empowering you to make dynamic and intelligent web applications through component determination, control, and occasion dealing with. This mix of innovations enables designers to make connecting with and easy to use web encounters.

Investigating and Mistakes Taking care of

In the realm of coding, troubleshooting and mistake dealing with are fundamental abilities for any software engineer or designer. These practices help recognize and determine issues as well as guarantee that the product you make moves along as expected. Normal Coding Missteps:

- Punctuation Mistakes: These are the most fundamental missteps where you could fail to remember a semicolon or incorrectly spell a variable name. Grammar blunders are normally simple to detect and fix.

- Coherent Blunders: These are trickier to distinguish as they don't necessarily toss mistakes. Coherent blunders happen when your code doesn't deliver the normal result because of imperfect calculations or wrong information taking care of.

- Variable Perusing: Abusing variable degree can prompt startling way of behaving. Factors pronounced worldwide may conflict with neighborhood factors, causing issues.

- Cluster and Record Blunders: Getting to a component of an exhibit that doesn't exist or utilizing a wrong record can prompt runtime blunders.

- Utilizing Program Engineer Apparatuses for Troubleshooting:
- Present day web improvement frequently includes troubleshooting JavaScript code in the program. Program engineer devices, like those in Chrome or Firefox, are strong guides in this cycle. You can set breakpoints, review factors, and step through your code to recognize and fix issues. These apparatuses likewise show mistake messages and control center logs to assist you with understanding what turned out badly.

Try...Catch for Mistake Dealing with in JavaScript:

JavaScript gives the try...catch explanation to strong mistake taking care of. This is the closely guarded secret:

```javascript
Duplicate code
attempt {
    // Code that could toss a mistake
} get (mistake) {
    // Code to deal with the mistake
}
```

You place the code that could toss a mistake inside the attempt block. In the event that a blunder happens, it's gotten, and the execution leaps to the catch block, where you can deal with the mistake nimbly. This is especially helpful for managing network demands, record I/O, or any activity that could fall flat.

In outline, dominating troubleshooting and blunder dealing with is significant for any coder. Understanding normal coding botches, using program engineer devices, and utilizing builds like try...catch in JavaScript will assist you with making more dependable and mistake-free programming. Everything really revolves around finding and fixing those bugs effectively to convey excellent code.

Stacking Outer Contents:

Stacking outside scripts is an essential piece of web improvement. It includes incorporating outer JavaScript records in your page. This should be possible in the HTML report utilizing the <script> tag with a sec quality that focuses to the outer content's URL. These contents can be facilitated on happy conveyance organizations (CDNs) or your own server. They empower you to expand the usefulness of your website page by consolidating pre-fabricated libraries or custom code.

Making AJAX Solicitations:

AJAX (Offbeat JavaScript and XML) is a procedure for making no concurrent solicitations to a server from a site page. This is vital for making dynamic and intelligent web applications. Journalists might view this as helpful to comprehend on the grounds that it's the innovation behind current web applications and can be a subject important to your peruses. AJAX demands are normally made utilizing JavaScript, permitting information to be recovered or shipped off a server without requiring a full page invigorate.

Dealing with Reactions from APIs:

APIs (Application Programming Connection points) are sets of decides and conventions that permit different programming applications to speak with one another. For an essayist and distributer, this is a critical theme, as APIs are utilized in a great many ventures. While making Programming interface demands, the reaction from the Programming interface can be in different configurations, like JSON or XML. Journalists might have to make sense of how for parse and utilize the information got back from APIs in their articles.

It's vital to stress that these subjects are interconnected. Stacking outer scripts frequently includes making AJAX solicitations to get those contents from a server. APIs are usually utilized for recovering information or performing activities on far off servers, and this frequently includes AJAX solicitations to send and get information.

1. let and const:

ES6 acquainted two new ways with proclaim factors: let and const. In contrast to the past var watchword, let and const have block-level degree, which forestalls variable spillage and accidental changes. const is utilized for proclaiming constants whose values can't be reassigned.

2. Bolt Works:

Bolt works give a compact linguistic structure to composing capabilities. They are particularly valuable for mysterious capabilities and proposition a more certain this limiting. For instance:

javascript
Duplicate code
const duplicate = (a, b) => a * b;
3. Layout Literals:
Layout literals permit you to make strings with installed articulations. This improves on string link and addition. You use backticks () to characterize layout literals, and placeholders are encased in ${}'.

javascript
Duplicate code
const name = "John";
const welcoming = 'Hi, ${name}! `;
4. Destructuring Task:
Destructuring permits you to extricate values from exhibits or items and allot them to factors. This can make code more succinct and decipherable.

javascript
Duplicate code
const [x, y] = [1, 2];// x = 1, y = 2

5. Classes:

ES6 presented class grammar for making items and characterizing constructors, techniques, and properties. It's a more organized method for working with items and models.

javascript
Duplicate code
```javascript
class Individual {
  constructor(name) {
    this.name = name;
  }
  welcome() {
    return 'Hi, my name is ${this.name}';
  }
}
```

6. Modules:

ES6 presented a module framework that permits you to import and product capabilities, classes, and factors. This advances measured quality in your code.

```javascript
Duplicate code
// Sending out
send out const add = (a, b) => a + b;

// Bringing in
import { add } from './math';
```

These are only a couple of the critical highlights of ES6. It carried numerous different enhancements to JavaScript, making it a more hearty and expressive language. ES6 has turned into the establishment for current JavaScript advancement and is generally taken on in both frontend and backend improvement.

Making a Specific Web Application with JavaScript

In the consistent old age, the ability to make web applications is a major end. Whether you're a writer or distributer wanting to resuscitate your web based presence or essentially someone shaky to get the hang of, building a key wise page can a splendid embrace. This guide will walk you through the imperative stages to make an irrefutable web application using JavaScript.

1. Setting Up Your Ceaseless situation:

Before we hop into the code, guarantee you have a substance

manager like Visual Studio Code or Grandiose Message presented on your PC. These editors offer a particularly arranged dash of relationship with making and managing your code.

2. HTML Improvement:

Each site page starts with HTML. Begin by making a HTML record, and inside it, portray the really design of your site page using HTML names. Here is an essential arrangement:

```
html
Copy code
<! DOCTYPE html>
<html>
<head>
```

```
 <!-- Your substance will go here - -
>
</body>
</html>
```

3. Adding JavaScript:

To add data to your page, you'll require JavaScript. Make one more satisfied name inside the HTML record's <head> district and join your JavaScript code:

html
Copy code

```
<script>
   // Your JavaScript code will go
here
</script>
```

4. Building Getting it:

We ought to add a central portrayal of sense. Expect you really need to make a button that changes the text when clicked. You can do this by picking a HTML part and changing its substance. Here is a model:

html
Copy code

```
<script>
    limit changeText() {

document.getElementById("content").innerHTML = "Text has been changed!";
    }
</script>
```

In addition, in the HTML body:

html
Copy code

5. Testing Your Web Application:

Open your HTML record in a web program to see your web application, considering everything. Tapping the button should change the text as portrayed in your JavaScript limit.

This is just a sprinkle of something more basic concerning web improvement. You can similarly in this manner associate with your web application by looking further into HTML, CSS for styling, and further made JavaScript strategy. The web is a giant resource for enlightening activities and documentation.

- "Clean Code: A Handbook of Nimble Programming Craftsmanship" by Robert C. Martin: This book underscores composing spotless, viable code, an important expertise for designers.

- "JavaScript: The Great Parts" by Douglas Crockford: Assuming that you're into web improvement, this book centers around the accepted procedures and great parts of JavaScript.

- "Configuration Examples: Components of Reusable Article Situated Programming" by Erich Gamma, Richard Steerage,

Ralph Johnson, and John Vlissides: This exemplary book dives into configuration designs, which are fundamental for programming advancement.

- Websites:

- Stack Flood: An important asset for engineers to seek clarification on pressing issues and track down replies to normal and complex issues.

- GitHub: A stage for facilitating and teaming up on code. It's an extraordinary spot to track down open-source projects, contribute, and team up with different designers.

- MDN Web Docs: Mozilla Engineer Organization gives exhaustive documentation on web advances, especially helpful for web designers.

- Online Courses:

- Coursera: Offers courses in different programming dialects, web improvement, and software engineering themes.

- edX: Gives courses from colleges and establishments on a great many specialized subjects.

- Udemy: Highlights a tremendous choice of

seminars on programming, web improvement, and programming.

Conclusion:

Sum up the key action items.
Urge amateurs to keep rehearsing and investigating JavaScript

Positively, how about we wrap up our conversation on JavaScript and urge amateurs to continue to improve their abilities in this flexible language.

JavaScript is a central programming language utilized broadly in web improvement. All through our discussion, we've investigated its key perspectives, including information types, capabilities, and the Report Item Model (DOM). Novices, as you adventure into the universe of coding with JavaScript, recollect a couple of key important points:

Versatility: JavaScript isn't only for web improvement. You can involve it for server-side prearranging (Node.js), portable application improvement, and, surprisingly, in the Web of Things (IoT).

Begin Basic: In the event that you're simply starting, center around the nuts and bolts. Comprehend factors, information types, and how to compose capabilities. These are the structure blocks of JavaScript.

DOM Authority: Figuring out how to control the DOM is significant for web advancement. It's the manner by which you make intuitive and dynamic pages.

Practice, Practice, Practice: Like any expertise, programming gets better with training. Compose code consistently, and go ahead and commit errors - that is the means by which you learn.

Investigate Structures and Libraries: As you progress, consider investigating famous JavaScript structures like Respond, Precise, or Vue, and libraries like jQuery. They can make your improvement assignments more effective.

Remain Refreshed: The universe of web improvement is continually developing. Stay aware of the most recent JavaScript highlights and best practices to remain pertinent in the field.